DEDIC

This book is dedicated to 1
Josiah Nedd [1935 – 2011]. F   ...spiration and
taught me so much about doing and being more.

Despite overcoming a number of personal obstacles including losing his mother, at a young age and surviving a horrific crash that destroyed his car and left his jaw wired I never saw him depressed or down.

He had a way of standing tall and strong despite being relatively small in stature but his personality filled a room, and he had an air of arrogance that was equally endearing and infuriating.

Today, almost five years after his passing I am proud to write this dedication to him because my journey has been similar to the one he took, and I'm proud to say that I'm his daughter.

The Cracked Cocoon

Roianne. C. C. Nedd

CONTENTS

ACKNOWLEDGMENTS

Although this is a self-help book, it wouldn't be right not to acknowledge some of the people who had pivotal roles in my development journey.

1. Miss Anderson – My English teacher. I gravitated to her from the first lesson she taught me. She emitted a warmth tinged with a strength that demanded respect. I guess she's a big part of why I enjoy reading and writing so much.

2. Mrs McGowan – She taught me French and with her help I was able to develop from being the "duncest" girl she had ever tried to teach French, to being one of the top of my class, exceeding my predicted exam grade by two levels.

3. Mrs Liverpool – My Office Procedure teacher. She opened her home to us for lessons and became someone who I loved and respected and who I still keep in touch with now.

4. Mrs Breedy – After a tumultuous first term studying accounts, her teaching style helped me stay on track and today I can proudly say that I'm a fully qualified Certified Chartered Accountant.

5. Danny Edet – My first line manager when I joined the UK Civil Service in 1999. He is a big part of why I stayed longer than the six months that I had originally planned.

6. Sean Rigney – Who I met when I was considering leaving the Civil Service. He offered me a job with an immediate start date and something made me accept, this led to me staying in service for almost another decade.

7. Garry Winder – For offering me a job opportunity that stretched me and gave me the opportunity to crack my Cocoon.

8. Jennifer Joseph – She showed me that Black women could progress higher than I first imagined.

9. Matt Egan – For being a great line manager and remaining a friend to this day.

10. Nick Smedley – A force of nature who was the first Senior Civil Servant that I worked closely with. He gave me many opportunities and was my first mentor and sponsor.

11. Kate Todman – An amazing programme manager who inspired me to become a qualified project manager.

12. Carolyn Batt – A consultant who taught me all about ethical management consultancy. This would later provide a blueprint for the way I ran my business.

13. Dan Colborne – One of my favourite line managers. I don't think I've ever had such a great advocate since.

14. Mary Shaw – a friend, a mentor, and inspiration. She taught me so much about politics on both a micro and a macro scale.

15. Carolyn Downs- She was an inspirational leader who advocated for women and showed me that the path to the top doesn't have to be paved with lots of academic achievements. Hard work and dedication are equally important.

What's Inside
The Cocoon?

INTRODUCTION

This book has been about four years in the making. The name came to me after a visit to a Butterfly exhibition, and I was optimistically sure that I would be able to write it in six months.

Maybe I hadn't had enough life experiences yet, or I wasn't totally ready because that six months dragged on and on and now we are here.

The aim of this book is to chart my journey to finding peace and contentment by pushing through the pain of change, smashing my comfort zone and Cracking my Cocoon. The book has ten sections that help you identify the stage of change that you are at and inspire you to persevere with making the change in your life.

So as I said I've been meaning to write this book for years because I've been Cracking my Cocoon for a while now.

"I'm living on borrowed time and I want to make it count!"

I'm constantly learning and evolving. Maybe it's because technically I shouldn't be here.

My mother had a difficult pregnancy and labour, and I'm sure that more than once there was a chance that I wouldn't survive. So in essence, I'm living my life on borrowed time, and I want to make it count.

Every time I thought that my life couldn't change anymore, it suddenly did, and the book got pushed to the bottom of my to-do list but o the bright side it gave me more to write about when I did finally finish the book.

The steps that I outline in this book aren't about a chronological journey nor are they steps that you only take once in your life.

The Cracked Cocoon is about a cycle, and you may only recognise some steps or a different order or even find that certain steps are repeated while others have never happened.

This is an individual journey, and there are no wrong answers. If it feels right, then it's right.

So, welcome to the world of the Cracked Cocoon where "change is the only constant".

WHY LISTEN TO ME?

I'm sure some of you will be wondering what makes me qualified to write this book. I'm not a psychologist, therapist or counsellor.

The thing that qualifies me is that I've had quite an eventful life, so I'm able to approach this with a "been there, done that" mentality.

I don't have all the answers, but more likely than not I've experienced the emotional turmoil that you may be going through right now. So my "qualifications" in no particular order:

Love
I have had two failed marriages and a few relationships as well. I understand heartbreak, and I know how to survive a broken heart. I've cried myself to sleep, lamented a lost love and lived in the world of "what if" far too many times.

"I don't have all the answers but I've had lots of experiences"

Life
I had a childhood that involved moving back and forth between Guyana and London. When I was 19 I was sexually assaulted. I lost a parent in my early 30's, and I had postnatal depression after I gave birth to my daughter.

Career
I've had numerous jobs and my career spans, the public, private and charitable sectors. I have worked hard to get professional recognition, and I have had periods of

unemployment and under-employment.

It hasn't been easy by any stretch of the imagination.

ARE YOU READY TO EMERGE?

A Cocoon is a safe place. It's your comfort zone and this process of cracking it is going to be uncomfortable.

The closest comparison I can make is pulling off a plaster. Some people do it slow, piece by piece leaving it hanging off their body while they muster the courage to take the next part off. Others rip it off quickly unconcerned with what might happen because they are so focused on moving onto the next part of the healing process. Then there are the inbetweeners. The people who do it slowly at the start and then end at a high speed.

"I still have doubts; I still have fears"

I am an in-betweener, I start off slow and then I rip it off at full speed. Personally, the first time I consciously felt my Cocoon start to Crack was when I found out that I was pregnant. Note that I said it started to crack. Your Cocoon, like mine, is unlikely to crack in a neat line. Life just isn't that simple.

So now, having created multiple cracks in my Cocoon I know that I'm ready to emerge. Don't get me wrong, I still have doubts; I still have fears. I still sometimes yearn for the comfort of my Cocoon, but I know that there is no going back. I went back once and although it was comfortable for a while it didn't assuage the urge for a change in my life. It didn't permanently take me off my true path.

Laid bare in this book is the journey that I took to Crack my Cocoon. It wasn't just one aspect of my life that required change it was a few so you will find references to all different things within these pages.

So back to the almost beginning. I was 25, when I found out that I was going to be a mother, and suddenly my world changed. Everything was different.
I had to change
My life had to change
And I had no clue what to do next.
All I knew was that I felt a yearning
A desire to Do More and Be More
I needed to Crack my Cocoon.

THE CRACKED COCOON CHECKLIST

Before you start to delve into this book, it is useful to do a quick check. Don't spend too long thinking about it and don't discount any answers that come to you instantaneously.

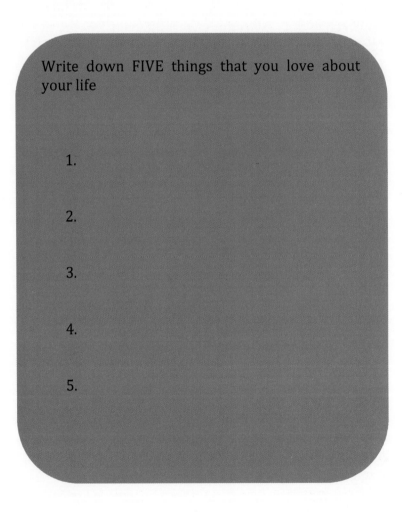

Write down FIVE things that you love about your life

1.

2.

3.

4.

5.

Write down THREE things that you want to change

1.

2.

3.

Great! You're ready!

Let's go!

It's time to WAKE up.

Awakening

AWAKENING

Have you ever had a feeling? A yearning for something more but you weren't sure what that something more was? That yearning is/was your awakening. It can take years for you to feel this way but it does exist. My yearning started when I was young. The calling of the entrepreneurial spirit was strong for me.

At age 5, I wrote my first book. It was a short but accurate autobiography. I can't explain or remember why I did it, but I do remember that the front cover had vivid orange and purple stripes that I was forced to recreate on multiple copies because I intended to sell them to various members of my family to maximise my profits. I sold them for 10p, a princely sum for a 5-year-old.

"Learn quick.

Fail fast!"

Looking back this was genuinely my awakening. There is no reason I should have been thinking about earning money, but yet, I was.

Both my parents had traditional jobs working for the Greater London Council (GLC). Maybe I had heard my father talking about this thing called business, but I couldn't know what it was. So this must have been my destiny. This was the Universe's first sign to me that I was born to be an entrepreneur. I was born to learn quick and fail fast. The qualities of a true entrepreneur.

Unsurprisingly, I didn't listen to that first call. How could I? I was five years old ready to embark on school life.

A few years later my father was made redundant from GLC and started his own finance and accountancy business which sparked another ambition in me. I recall sitting under my father's desk pretending to be an accountant. I wasn't sure what it meant but knowing that it would involve papers and numbers was enough for me.

I was an overachiever at school and excelled academically from day one. Although being an accountant was one of my ambitions it wasn't a calling. All I ever wanted to do was be me.

But actually, there was an awakening for me all those years ago, but I missed it. My calling was and is to be a writer.

AWAKENING REVIEW

So let's see if you missed anything ...

What did you want to be when you were younger?

What did you want to be when you were younger?

What are you doing now? Write a brief
summary of your life up to this point .....

Think about your answers.

If you aren't doing anything remotely related to what
you used to want to be or to what you enjoyed when
you were younger then maybe you missed the signs of
your awakening, or it came later in life.

If, however you still yearn for something related to
these memories then maybe you have just been
AWAKENED!

Awareness

The moment that something catches your attention, but you don't know why

AWARENESS

Awareness comes when you make a decision that is based on the message that you are being given. A real, proper, life altering decision. With all these messages about entrepreneurialism hitting me every few years you probably expect to hear that I was a child prodigy, making my first million by 21 but I wasn't. Don't underestimate how hard it can be to answer your true calling.

"It can be hard to follow your true calling"

The first time I gave that message any attention was when I was 14. I had to make a decision about which classes I wanted to take as part of my CXC (Caribbean O-Level) exams. I remember that I knew I was going to choose the business stream. There was never any doubt for me that I had absolutely no interest in doing something scientific. I wanted to do business plain and simple.

I remember speaking to my father about it and he asked me why I wanted to do business. I don't remember what I said to him or much of the discussion but I know that I was allowed to go into the business stream. I spoke to my mother about it too. She had studied business and with Daddy being an accountant, at least, I knew I would have support at home.

I was good at most of my subjects although I initially struggled with Accounting until Mrs Breedy, started to teach me and it all suddenly made sense.

Other teachers who made a difference to me during

those years were Miss Anderson my English teacher and Mrs McGowan my French teacher. She helped me to catch up on French after I moved from London to Guyana. A fact many people don't know is that I only did half of my second year at secondary school because we moved from London to Guyana.

So during the six months before I started in my third year, I soaked up lots of books. First from my mother's shelf, where Maya Angelou was my favourite. I read all of her works and then started on my father's shelf.

There I found strong words from Martin Luther King Jnr, Gandhi, Salman Rushdie and finally Malcolm X, a story that had also been made into a movie that year. I learnt a lot from those books in those months.

> *"I couldn't avoid the lure of entrepreneurialism"*

Living in Guyana gave me a new perspective on entrepreneurial spirit. Everywhere I turned there was someone doing their thing, earning a dollar trying their hand at business. This included both of my parents. My mother ran a catering company, and my father was doing property management and financial planning as well as having a stationery supply shop.

All the businesses were run out of our three-storey home with accompanying office building behind the house so I couldn't avoid the lure of entrepreneurialism. Not that I would have wanted to. Like the times before I was immersed in the family businesses. I understood income and expenditure because of my burgeoning studies in accountancy and I sometimes even helped to type documents so that I could practice for my typewriting exam.

To this day over 20 years later, I do not regret going into the business stream. Yes, when I think about the current STEM (Science, Technology, Engineering and Mathematics) skills shortages I wonder if maybe I should have tried something different but in my heart, I know I made the right choice. And there is an important lesson to be learnt from my decision. When you follow your passion, you will *"I followed my passion"* have the mental strength and desire to succeed. I achieved the following results in my exams two years after making that choice:

Principles of Accounts – A*
Principles of Business – A*
Office Procedures – A*
English Language – A*
English Literature – A*
Social Studies – A*
Mathematics A*
French – Grade 1 (A)
Typewriting – Grade 2 (B)

Looking back, I believe that I achieved those results, making me one of the top ten students in the country because I followed my passion and answered the call of the universe.

So how do you become more aware? Awareness is about examining and studying your life.

You have to reflect.

REFLECTION

Take some time to look at the patterns in your life an answer the following questions.

Do you always end up in the same type of role in an organisation even when that isn't the formal role that you applied for? Do you gravitate to certain tasks?

> What type of job do you usually do? Describe it in at least 5 words:
>
> 1.
> 2.
> 3.
> 4.
> 5.

If your issue is more relationship focused, do you always end up with the same "type" of partner? Not necessarily the same physical type it's about behaviours and mannerisms. The things that you only know when you get to know a person.

> Describe your "usual" type of partner in at least 5 words:
>
> 1.
> 2.
> 3.
> 4.
> 5.

Do you always end up leaving jobs/relationships for the same or similar reasons? Issues with the boss? Conflicts of interest?

Describe the reason(s) why you left your last job(s)/relationship(s) ....

Your life patterns are usually the universe giving you a sign. You just need to be AWARE!

Apathy
&
Anger

Apathy and Anger are two closely related stages. Some people experience one, or the other. On the other hand, some people experience them both. Either way, you are unlikely to avoid them.

APATHY

This is a stage that I have experienced frequently. It is the moment when I realise that something is wrong, but I can't muster the enthusiasm to fix it. So I accept it in its flawed nature and rather than move on I complain. That is how apathy is characterised for me, lots and lots of complaining.

I remember a few years ago I was working in a role that I no longer found challenging. I thought that I had accepted the non-challenging nature of the role, and I thought I would settle into a robotic bliss of not having to use too much brain power to deliver my job.

> *"I thought I was happy in my Cocoon"*

But I was wrong. Things started to niggle at me. I wanted to try different things and the more I found myself hemmed in or curtailed by my superiors, the more I moaned to anyone who would listen. But what I didn't do was try to find a new job or change my circumstances. I was happy in my Cocoon. Or so I thought.

I can only stay in the apathetic mode for a brief amount of time. After a while, I move quickly to the next phase! Over the page you can consider whether you are in the Apathy stage.

RECOGNISING APATHY

I have found that the apathy stage is often characterised by at least one or more of these three states, self-sabotage, procrastination and regret. Let's consider them in turn.

Self – Sabotage

This is where the voice in your head lives. The voice that tells you
    a. You aren't good enough
    b. You can't do it
    c. It's too hard

If any of these sound familiar you may be self-sabotaging.

Procrastination

Procrastination is a form of self-sabotage. How many of you have said that you will get around to making that job application and then before you know it the date has passed.

> *"Procrastination robs you of success"*

Another scenario is the person who always waits until "Monday" to make a change in their life. This procrastination often means that the change will never happen.

Regret

Regret is generally caused by self-sabotage and procrastination. How many of you have self-sabotaged or procrastinated and then spent time regretting and lamenting that the change you wanted hasn't happened?

Do you recognise any of the signs of apathy in your life? What are they? ....

ANGER

Apathy and Anger are interchangeable and intrinsically linked. Some people get angry because they can't make a decision, or they get angry because their procrastination leads to regret.

Alternatively, Anger can be a sign that something in your current situation is at odds with your core values.

Values are the things that create your unique code of life. They are the things that are fundamental to the way you live your life, and they are of utmost importance to you.

24 Common values and traits that people value or desire include:

- Respect	- Love
- Integrity	- Creativity
- Acceptance	- Challenge
- Fairness	- Intellect
- Honesty	- Consistency
- Inquisitiveness	- Determination
- Transparency	- Humility
- Mindfulness	- Caution
- Ambition	- Encouragement
- Optimism	- Flexibility
- Hard work	- Graciousness
- Reflection	- Harmony

Now you have seen the list go back and highlight the ones that mean the most to you.

Any surprises?

When one of my core values is questioned, I get angry. Think about the fight or flight response that humans have. Apathy is a flight response, and Anger is a fight response. Most of us have a natural preference for either of them. My common response is fight, so I tend to get angry when I am frustrated.

Think about various situations that you find yourself in. Do you lean towards fight or flight? Record your answer in the box below

> When I am in a frustrating situation I tend to .....
> _____

As we all know, Anger is viewed as a negative emotion but in some ways, Anger is your friend. Anger can galvanise you to make a change. Anger can help you stand up and take a blow at the shell of your Cocoon and can be the first step to cracking it.

WHAT DOES ANGER LOOK LIKE?

Are you ever sitting at work and you feel annoyed about being passed over for a promotion or development opportunity?

Do you ever feel like you don't have the life that you deserve?

Do you feel jealous or resentful of the achievements of others?

If you answered yes to any of these questions, then you may be in the Angry stage, and it is time to use that anger to move forward.

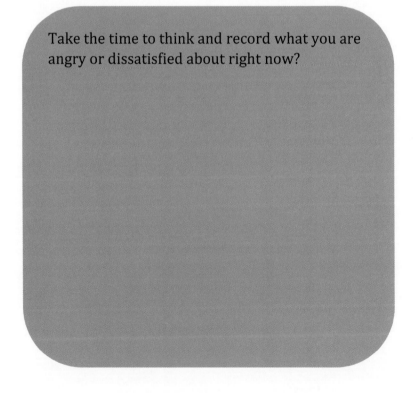

Take the time to think and record what you are angry or dissatisfied about right now?

Acknowledgment

ACKNOWLEDGMENT

This stage is when you finally stop, take a breath and listen to what your heart and soul are telling you. It is now that you understand that there are clear messages urging you to do something.

You don't yet know what needs to change, but you are acknowledging that all is not well in your world. In a way, this is the "red or blue pill" moment (for Matrix fans).

Acknowledgment is one of my least favourite stages. It requires high levels of self-awareness, patience and openness. I am very self-aware, but sometimes I don't want to hear the message.

"Your intuition protects you"

One of the hardest areas of life to use the acknowledgement stage on is relationships. Let me give you an example from my life. A few years ago I was in a relationship with someone who used to be my friend. It was intense, it was good, but sometimes my mind niggled. Sometimes his stories and excuses didn't add up, but I wasn't ready to acknowledge my gut.

I committed the cardinal sin. I ignored my intuition. Your intuition exists to protect you and send you signals, but many people do not recognises these signs or simply ignore them.

So here I was in this seemingly great relationship, but sometimes I just felt like something was wrong. Sometimes I wanted more and sometimes I didn't trust him. I would almost hear my subconscious whisper the words; he's lying to me as he recounted another tale of woe or another story about something that wasn't his fault.

Later I found out that he had some issues, the biggest being that he was manipulative and narcissistic. Our relationship was doomed from the moment I asked him to consider my feelings. He was selfish and demanding and drained all my energy when he was around. I even started to call him my energy vampire.

"Listen to your subconscious"

Despite these signs it took me over a year to acknowledge the predictable demise of the relationship.

The thing about acknowledgment is that once you start to listen to the signs and acknowledge that there is more than meets the eye the cracks start to appear and your mind will not rest until you have investigated and it is that investigation that leads to ACCEPTANCE.

Acceptance

ACCEPTANCE

I figured out last year that I am a creative soul. Despite self-sabotaging and listening to that voice that told me I couldn't and shouldn't I shook off the shackles and embraced my creativity.

Once I accepted it I wrote and published book after book, and I even started painting and showing my work. It is something I never thought I would be able to do, but here I am writing and painting as well as working on the intellectual stuff that I've always had a knack for.

Anyway, back to you. You've finally accepted that all is not well in your little cosy Cocoon. Your mind and your gut are in alignment. You know that something needs to change but maybe you aren't sure what needs to change.

Or maybe you know exactly what area of their life they need to focus on. Either way, it's time to take stock. Out with the old and in with the new. It's time to do the Change Inventory.

"I embraced my creativity"

Over the next few pages, you will analyse ten areas in your life and assess how satisfied you are with those areas. An explanation of the scoring is included.

CHANGE INVENTORY

The Change Inventory, is a practical way for you to consider which area of your life may lead to a Cracked Cocoon moment.

It is particularly useful if you feel the Awareness and Awakening but aren't sure why.

Rate each area from 0 to 10 with 10 being most satisfied and 0 being most dissatisfied. Below each heading there are challenge questions to help you think about your score.

Life Area	Score	Notes
Career Do you like your job? Are you doing the job that you always wanted to do? Do you enjoy going to work?		
Finances Do you have debt? Are you struggling to make ends meet? Would you like to earn more? Would you like to spend less?		
Health and Wellbeing Do you have any health conditions that impair your quality of life? Do you feel stressed? Do you feel depressed? Would you like to change your weight/appearance?		

Life Area	Score	Notes
Friends and Family Think about these relationships, are any of them fractured? Do you need to reconcile with anyone? Do you need to distance yourself from anyone?		
Love and Romance Are you happy with your relationship status? If you are in a relationship are you happy with your partner?		
Physical Environment Are you happy with your home? Its location, size, décor?		
Qualifications Do you feel fully qualified? Are there more qualifications or certifications that you would like to get?		
Fun and Relaxation Do you get enough downtime? When last did you take a break? What do you do to relax? Do you have a hobby?		
Sense of Self		

Life Area	Score	Notes
Are you fulfilled? Do you feel like you know who you are? Do you feel like you are still finding yourself?		
Spirituality Do you believe in a power higher than yourself? Have you explored this belief? Are you comfortable with your spiritual journey or lack thereof if you have no belief?		

Interpreting Your Answers

1. Look at your responses.
2. Consider any area that scored less than 5.
3. Is that a score that you want to improve?
4. If you want to improve it, that is one of your Cracked Cocoon priorities
5. If you don't want to improve it, then move on and don't give it another thought

Aspiration

The most important component of aspiration is self-belief. To aspire to be anything you first have to believe that you can achieve it.

ASPIRATION

Self-belief is very difficult to achieve and sustain. One of my sayings is "You have to fake it till you feel it" because it won't always come naturally. To help build my confidence I use affirmations.

Affirmations are phrases that you use to give you confidence. They are used repetitively and work best when said aloud although I have had success with saying them in my head.

My very first affirmation was "I am the shit" it doesn't sound particularly positive but for me it meant that I was cute and that I was invincible. I even had a walk that went with it. My hips would swing in time to the syllables of the affirmation. It worked for me although I never said it out loud.

"Fake it till you feel it"

These days my affirmations are more specific. I believe that you breathe positivity into your life by saying the things that you want and need in your life and allowing them to manifest themselves.

I'm not saying that it's easy to have belief, but I try. It takes work and dedication to believe in myself. But I'm worth it and so are YOU.

On the next page are four examples of how affirmations have manifested themselves in my life.

Manifestation 1

When my daughter was a baby I had lots of debt and high childcare fees. I was struggling month to month. It was January and I had been paid early in December because of Christmas. My daughter needed nappies and milk and I had three days to go till payday and didn't want to ask anyone for help.

I went to the ATM hoping that one of my accounts had £10.00 in it. There was a man in front of me but I didn't pay him any mind. He did his transaction then it was my turn. As I got to the front £130 came out. I called to the man but he didn't turn or respond.

I quickly checked my balance while keeping an eye out for where the man had gone. He was walking very slowly. I had no money in my account. I grabbed my card and hustled to catch up with the man so that I could give him his money. I saw him go into a small shop with only one entrance and exit. I hurried into the shop to find the man had disappeared. There were no customers in the shop and the shop keeper hadn't seen anyone.

Manifestation 2

It was almost time for me to graduate but the ceremony was a week before payday. I wanted to get my hair done so the pictures would look nice but I didn't have any extra money. It was going to cost me £60.

I was on my way to see a friend via the underground (subway) I took a seat because I was early when suddenly I saw a purple flash on the floor. The wind was merrily blowing a £20 note around in front of me. I got up and grabbed it.

As I walked back to my seat I saw another purple flash. There in the crease where I had previously been sitting were two more £20 notes. I now had exactly £60.

Manifestation 3

I was unexpectedly required to travel out of London for work and would need to take two taxis. Company policy was to pay you after you had spent the money. I was broke.

I kept thinking if I had £50 it would tide me over until payday which was in five days. It was on my mind as I didn't want to ask for help.

As I walked between my house and my mother's house to pick up my daughter I looked down at my feet and saw something red. I bent to pick it up and found a folded £50 note.

Manifestation 4

Recently I spent a month with no form of income. All my major contracts were done and I was struggling to find work. Those four weeks felt like an eternity.

I have worked since I was a teenager and it felt so alien to me. To help me get through this period I developed the affirmation

"I have a job, everything will be ok"

I said it out loud maybe ten to twenty times a day and when I least expected it I was offered a job and called for three interviews within one week.

FIND YOUR AFFIRMATION

Developing your own affirmations is a fairly easy process. Follow these steps to develop yours.

1. Use positive words. Like CAN and WILL.
2. Avoid framing things in the negative such as I can't, or I won't
3. Be specific. Saying "I want to be rich" is unlikely to create a manifestation.

Here are some examples of affirmations that you could use and tweak to your needs.

❖ *I am happy, and I am healthy*
[this is a reminder affirmation]

❖ *I am financially secure*
[although this isn't specific it allows you to be secure rather than citing a number which may fluctuate depending on circumstances]

❖ *I am enough*
[sometimes affirmations can be used to quell self-doubt]

❖ *I am beautiful*
[this is an affirmation that can build self-esteem]

❖ *I will be ok*
[this affirmation soothes worry]

❖ *I can do this*
[a good short term affirmation relating to a task]

❖ *I will succeed*
[useful for exams or tests]

Action

So you are ready to change something in your life. You're ready for action. So now my accountancy background kicks in. Exactly what do you want to achieve? It is time to create an action plan.

ACTION

There are so many ways to plan for the change in your life. This chapter presents one of the ways.

First you need to know that you have all it takes to make this change.

Your skills and experiences are your tools. These form the building blocks of any change that you need to make.

So let's start building!

Write at least three things that you are good at ..

Write about something that you are proud of ......

> Write about a lesson that you have learnt in life ...

Now you need to strengthen the foundations for your Cracked Cocoon Moment. To help you I have prepared the Action Plan Survey with ten questions for you to consider with space over the page to write your answers down.

1. What change are you trying to achieve?
2. When do you want to achieve it by?
3. Why haven't you made this change in the past?
4. Who can and will support you to make this change?
5. What support do you need?
6. On a scale of 0 to 10 with 10 being the most and 0 being the least. How much do you want to achieve this change?
7. What are you going to do today that will help you make that change
8. What are you going to do tomorrow to help you achieve that goal
9. What will you be doing next month to achieve the change or live with the change?
10. How are you going to feel when you achieve that change?

ACTION PLAN SURVEY

The first thing you need to consider is what you are trying to achieve. Write it down in the box below.

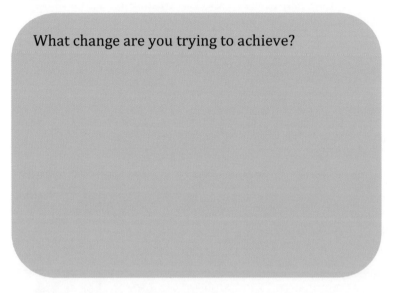

What change are you trying to achieve?

Knowing when you want the change to happen gives your mind focus. Write it in time e.g. within six months or write a date e.g. January 2017.

When do you want to achieve it by?

It is useful to reflect on why you haven't made this change in the past. Identify potential pitfalls and make plans for managing them this time around.

For instance, whenever I decide to lose weight I always consider what went wrong the last time. Was it the food in the house already or was it birthday season in the family? Think about what might derail you.

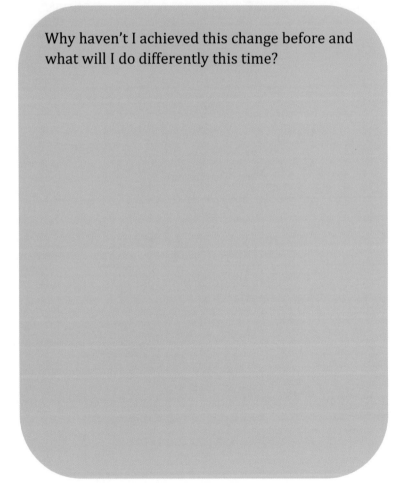

Why haven't I achieved this change before and what will I do differently this time?

The people around you can have a significant impact on your ability to make the change that you want. If you are changing the way you eat then you may have to think about how other people in the house eat. If you are planning a career change or gaining a qualification, you may need financial support. Most changes require you to have some support even if it's just someone to cheer you on. In the box below write down whose support you need and what you need from them.

Whose support do you need to make the change and what do you need from them?

On a scale of 0 to 10 with 0 being the least and 10 being the most how much do you want to achieve this change?

Change doesn't just happen. It takes work and commitment. Procrastination is one of the reasons that people fail at change and is my biggest vice. I am always waiting until tomorrow or until the start of a new week to effect the change. Don't be like me. Seize the day today and start making the change.

What are you going to do today that will help you make that change?

What are you going to do tomorrow that will help you make that change?

What will you be doing ONE month from now to help you achieve or be living with that change?

Visioning is an important part of achieving a change in your life. It is useful to think about how that change is going to make you feel. Will you be happy, content, proud. What does achieving the change mean for you?

How are you going to feel when you achieve that change?

Achievement

ACHIEVEMENT

Depending upon your personality type this stage can actually be quite difficult. How do you know that you have successfully Cracked your Cocoon?

I am the type of person who always wants more. I remember that my mentor and dear friend Mary used to tell me "know when good, is good enough". It is a concept that I struggle with. I am always looking for something more and think that there is something else.

With qualifications in accountancy, leadership, beauty, coaching and soon education, you would think that I

"Don't delay self - congratulation"

would stop but my current dreams include qualifying in nutrition, and I'm potentially considering formalising my HR qualifications, and my mind keeps turning slightly towards a Ph.D.!

But! The fact that I have recognised those achievements mean that I have successfully passed through this stage.

I know I will be here again, taking the time to reflect on another achievement, but right now I am focused on what I've already done. It is crucial that you recognise your achievements. Don't delay self-congratulation!

To help you reflect on your achievement(s), I have created the Certificate of Achievement template on the next page.

Certificate of Achievement

Awarded to

_____

On

_____

For

Write what you have achieved below

So how will you know when you have achieved what you set out to do?

Here are some tips.

1. If you didn't create an action plan in the Action part of the book, then do it now. Even if it is just a list of the things, you need to do and achieve. By creating a list, you can tell when you're done because everything on the list will be checked off.

2. If you change your mind midway on the journey about what you want, then accept that by discounting an option you have in essence Cracked your Cocoon. You are done with that topic or issue. You can mark it off your list.

3. Follow your instincts. Whether you know it or not that is the best marker. If you feel more free, lighter, in touch with your values and fulfilled. It means that you have Cracked your Cocoon.

Motivation
&
Inspiration

There are going to be days and times when it feels too hard to achieve the change that you want. In this section, I have included 100 inspirational quotes and comments to keep you going.

1. Success takes planning and planning takes patience. Think about what you want to achieve and set your intentions.

2. Approach your life as if there are no limits to your capabilities.

3. Activism sometimes creeps up on you by stealth. As your sense of being strengthens, the desire to be a role model grows.

4. When you open your eyes and see the world in all its hues is when you get what's meant for you.

5. The most important ingredient in self-improvement and empowerment is confidence. Self-doubt will derail you.

6. Everything in life is about choice. Even when you are forced to do something, you can choose to be gracious.

7. It's easy to be inspirational when you are up. What takes work is inspiring others when you're down.

8. Sexiness is a state of mind and happiness is a choice.

9. Serendipity comes to those who see it.

10. Seizing the day is not enough. You must focus, work, achieve and then celebrate.

11. Force yourself to smile no matter how you feel. Pretend you're happy until it's so.

12. The feeling of satisfaction from being productive should never be underestimated.

13. What is your weakness? Reflect, learn and improve.

14. What do you stand for? Try writing your personal manifesto. Be your own hero.

15. To grow, we must visit our past. Past skills and experiences shape us as humans and as leaders give us a strategic edge.

16. There is only one day of rest. So do something productive every other day.

17. Before you look at another in envy, stop and think. You don't know their journey. Focus on the positives in your life.

18. My happiness is defined by, lived by and enjoyed by, ME. Your happiness is different. No two roads to happy are paved the same way.

19. A person who helps themselves s more likely to receive help than the one who sits waiting for assistance.

20. What are you going to do to make your mark today?

21. Make your own future and blaze your own trail. Remember the only constant is change.

22. It's best to remember that though you may plan and aims and goals are great. You must always leave space for the unexpected.

23. Do good things come to those who wait? Or is it about getting up and grabbing opportunities?

24. How do you feed your passion? Do you even know what it is?

25. Use the summer to recharge your batteries and re-evaluate your dreams.

26. What difference is your existence going to make to the world?

27. Be about progress.

28. You owe it to yourself to be selfish sometimes. Chase your dreams, not someone else's!

29. Life isn't always gonna be easy, isn't always gonna be happy, but that's just life!

30. When last did you do something different? Change things up and be EXTRAordinary.

31. Feeding your passion is not an easy task nor is it something to take lightly. Live your dream and invest in your future.

32. Let's try the time travel exercise. What did you want to be when you were little? Have you achieved it? Reclaim your dream.

33. As you bask in the sunlight, take a moment to enjoy it and then consider how you can create a light for someone else to bask in.

34. Every day you create the history that your children will recount to theirs. Make yours a story that they are truly proud of.

35. Take a deep breath, reflect on your achievements and congratulate yourself for all that you have done

36. When you choose to share your talents for free, the appropriate reward follows naturally

37. Achieving your potential isn't always about doing something new or innovative. Sometimes it's just about doing your best.

38. Striving for answers in the complexity of life can be tiring but don't give up. There are answers to all of your questions.

39. Maybe yesterday didn't go the way that you thought it would. Don't let one bad day pull you away from your goals.

40. It's not the 1st of January, but this could be a fresh start. Make it day 1 of something fabulous.

41. If the only constant is change. Then evolution is necessary. Don't get stuck in a rut.

42. Failure isn't always the end. Sometimes it's the chance to pause, regroup and reassess what you want!

43. Any change you want to make requires a plan. Plan today change tomorrow.

44. When you take control of your life moving out of your comfort zone becomes easier.

45. Change is a long and winding journey. Sometimes you end up at a dead end, but no one said you couldn't reverse.

46. Treat today like a blank canvas. Every action is a brush stroke, fresh and new, leaving the worries of yesterday in the past.

47. Sexiness is a state of mind, not a state of being.

48. Do you believe in serendipity? Positive things happen to positive people. Think change, feel change, be change!

49. Do you know how it feels to be in the throes of inspiration? Who is your muse?

50. How do you capture your moments of clarity? Start writing them down!

51. Self-sufficiency is good but do not become immersed in solitude. Everyone needs someone else at some time in their life.

52. Great opportunities don't happen by chance; sometimes we create them!

53. Did you stick to your New Year's resolution? Don't worry, make the change now!

54. People complain that changing their lives is too difficult, too much or too soon. So I say, change the little things first.

55. How do you know what your dream is? Let today be the day that you listen to your heart.

56. How many of us blame others for our unhappiness? Well, it's no one else's responsibility to make you happy. Take control!

57. Have you ever taken a moment to ask yourself what you want to do with your life? What do you dream about?

58. Today is a great day to make a change whether small or big.

59. Seize the opportunity. The only failure is regret! Try things at least once rather than saying what if?

60. Today is as good as any to make the change you've been planning for so long.

61. The opposite of progress is not resistance but rather apathy. Because resistance takes effort but apathy leads to inertia.

62. Leadership is nothing without people who are willing to follow you. Do you lead or do you manage?

63. When you see, serendipity, don't ignore it. Embrace it.

64. To achieve we must keep moving, progress comes from continuous movement and continuous improvement.

65. Action, change, inspire, evolve, these are the tools to help you evolve.

66. It's not just about seizing the day it's about strategising and implementing. Bad planning leads to wasted time and energy.

67. Today I have purpose,
    Today I have faith,
    Today I will achieve
    Because forever I believe.

68. Positive thinking does not happen by chance. It takes effort, seeing beyond your current reality to identify the possibility.

69. Success is not defined by your wins. Every time you fail, you'll learn how talented you are. Happy failing.

70. Authenticity is free and takes less effort – Being you makes you more efficient.

71. Out of the ordinary comes the extraordinary.

72. Music creates a perfect backdrop for life. Choose your tune and create your new reality.

73. Stop. Breathe. Contemplate. Decide. Activate. Steps for achieving change.

74. I never said it was easy nor did I say it was hard. It's just the way it has to be, so that you can be, all you want to be.

75. If everyone were the same, we would all get lost. Find yourself. Be different.

76. The joy comes in achieving something new and learning what you never knew you didn't know.

77. Push out of your comfort zone. Stretch, feel and break free of the ties of routine.

78. As time ebbs and flows so do your dreams. Don't drown under drudgery.

79. Creativity unlocks productivity. Do something creative today.

80. Identify your values and fight for your beliefs.

81. Your skills are your currency. Use them for good and make wise investments.

82. Hard work only pays off if you know what you're working for.

83. Happiness is transient; contentment isn't. Strive for enough, not abundance.

84. No dream is too big, and no dream is too small. Your dreams are perfect for you.

85. The most important vow you can make is one to yourself. Be someone who you can trust.

86. Love easily, trust sensibly, live fully.

87. Complaining achieves nothing except exacerbating frustration. Make your change today.

88. Beauty is a unique trait that we all have.

89. Procrastination is like a comfort blanket. Cosy and warm but ultimately holding you back.

90. Your life is like a movie. Use your mouth as your speaker and your mind as a camera then make sure what you do is worthy of an award.

91. Avoid criticising yourself. You can always find critics but may struggle to find fans.

92. Everything you need is somewhere within you. Do an inventory today and discover the tools that you have.

93. When last did you do something new? Do something different today!

94. You can't achieve if you don't believe. Have faith and take the plunge.

95. Possessions may come and go, but memories last forever.

96. No battery lasts forever. Take time out and recharge yours regularly.

97. What makes you happy? Do it today.

98. Know when to be reflective and when to be reactive.

99. Jump in with both feet. You can't truly experience something with one foot outside the door.

100.   Live ~ Laugh ~ Love

ABOUT THE AUTHOR

Roianne Nedd is an experienced coach and equality and inclusion expert. She is passionate about self-improvement and the enrichment of others and has dedicated much of her free time to mentoring and helping people to achieve their dreams.

With a range of personal and professional experience, she brings real life examples to her work and a depth of empathy that belies her years.

The Cracked Cocoon is her first self-help book and represents a pivotal point in her journey as a life coach. Through this book her quirky yet effective brand of coaching can be accessed by many.

Visit www.roijelly.co.uk for more information and follow her on twitter @RC3Change

ABOUT THE PUBLISHER

ROI JELLY Publishing was established in December 2014 to work with writers who have a story to tell but want to retain control of their work.

We work with our writers to provide a bespoke publishing service that meets their needs and budgets.

We are anxious to hear from writers from across the world to discuss how we can help make their work go global. We are also passionate about bringing social issues to light and support various causes.

Email us at roijelly@outlook.com
Visit us at www.roijelly.co.uk/wepublish

Printed in Great Britain
by Amazon

12519486R00054